STRUM Together

CHRISTMAS SONGS

PREFACE

Learning to play a musical instrument is one of the most satisfying experiences a person can have. Being able to play along with other musicians makes that even more rewarding. This collection of Christmas songs is designed to make it easy to enjoy the fun of gathering with friends and family to make music together.

The music for each song displays the chord diagrams for five instruments: ukulele, baritone ukulele, guitar, mandolin and banjo. The chord diagrams indicate basic, commonly used finger positions. More advanced players can substitute alternate chord formations.

WITHDRAWN

D1452235

ISBN: 978-1-5400-2948-5

HAL•LEONARD®

Visit Hal Leonard Online at
www.halleonard.com

Contact Us:
Hal Leonard
7777 West Bluemound Road
Milwaukee, WI 53213
Email: info@halleonard.com

In Europe contact:
Hal Leonard Europe Limited
Distribution Centre, Newmarket Road
Bury St Edmunds, Suffolk, IP33 3YB
Email: info@halleonardeurope.com

In Australia contact:
Hal Leonard Australia Pty. Ltd.
4 Lentara Court
Cheltenham, Victoria, 3192 Australia
Email: info@halleonard.com.au

Tuning

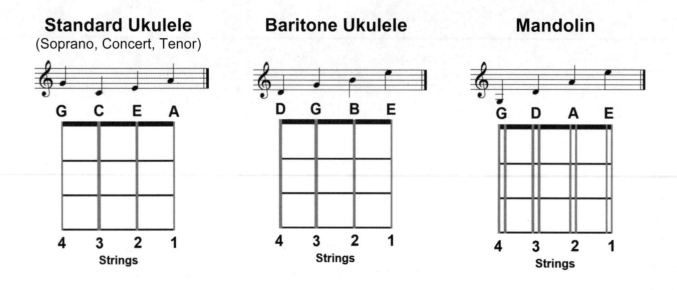

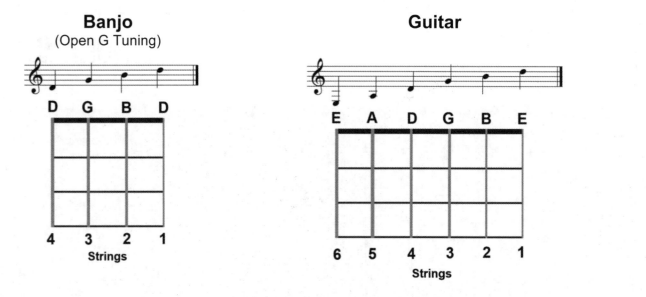

All banjo chord formations illustrated in this book are based on "Open G" tuning. If an alternate tuning is used the banjo player can read the chord letters for the songs and disregard the diagrams.

CONTENTS

Standard Ukulele

G	D	E	Am	C	D 7
			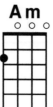		

Baritone Ukulele

G	D	E	Am	C	D 7
		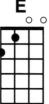			

Guitar

G	D	E	Am	C	D 7
				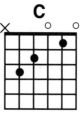	

Mandolin

G	D	E	Am	C	D 7
	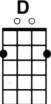		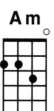		

Banjo

G	D	E	Am	C	D 7

Angels We Have Heard on High

Traditional French Carol
Translated by James Chadwick

Verse

1. An - gels we have heard on high sweet - ly sing - ing o'er the plains.
2. Shep - herds, why this ju - bi - lee? Why your joy - ous strains pro - long?
3. Come to Beth - le - hem and see Him whose birth the an - gels sing.
4. See with - in a man - ger laid Je - sus, Lord of heav'n and earth!

And the moun - tains in re - ply, ech - o back their joy - ous strains.
Say, what may the tid - ings be which in - spire your heav'n - ly song?
Come a - dore on bend - ed knee Christ the Lord, the new - born King.
Mar - y, Jo - seph, lend your aid, with us sing our Sav - ior's birth.

Chorus

Glo - ri - a

in ex - cel - sis De - o. Glo -

- ri - a in ex - cel - sis De - o. o.

Standard Ukulele

G	C	D 7	D
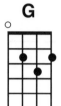	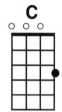		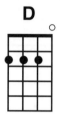

Baritone Ukulele

G	C	D 7	D
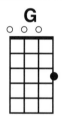	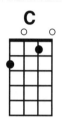	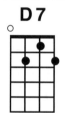	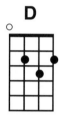

Guitar

G	C	D 7	D
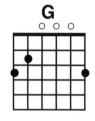	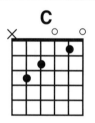	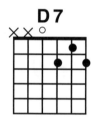	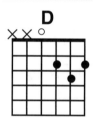

Mandolin

G	C	D 7	D
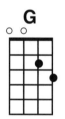	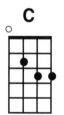	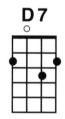	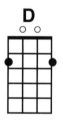

Banjo

G	C	D 7	D
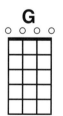	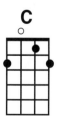	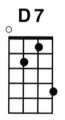	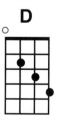

As with Gladness Men of Old

Words by William Chatterton Dix
Music by Conrad Kocher

Standard Ukulele

G   **D 7**   **C**   **A m**   **B 7**   **E m**

Baritone Ukulele

G   **D 7**   **C**   **A m**   **B 7**   **E m**

Guitar

G   **D 7**   **C**   **A m**   **B 7**   **E m**

  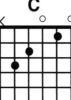 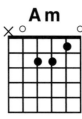 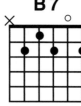 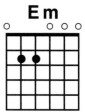

Mandolin

G   **D 7**   **C**   **A m**   **B 7**   **E m**

 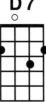 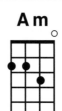

Banjo

G   **D 7**   **C**   **A m**   **B 7**   **E m**

Auld Lang Syne

Words by Robert Burns
Traditional Scottish Melody

Verse

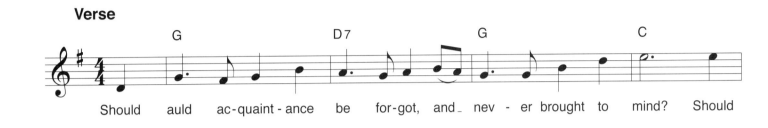

Chorus

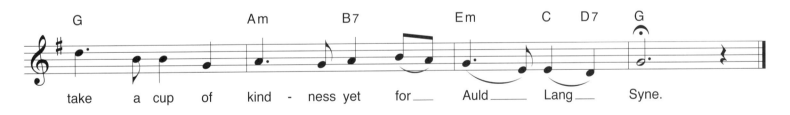

Standard Ukulele

G  **C** 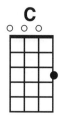 **D 7**  **A m**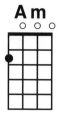

Baritone Ukulele

G 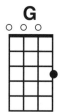 **C**  **D 7** 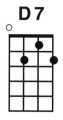 **A m**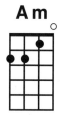

Guitar

G 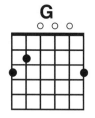 **C** 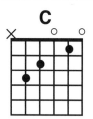 **D 7** 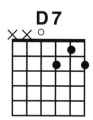 **A m**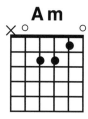

Mandolin

G 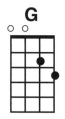 **C** 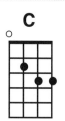 **D 7** 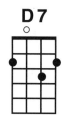 **A m**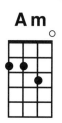

Banjo

G 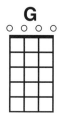 **C**  **D 7** 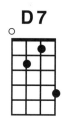 **A m**

Away in a Manger

Words by John T. McFarland (v.3)
Music by James R. Murray

Standard Ukulele

G	D7	G7	C	A7	C#°7
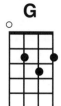		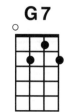	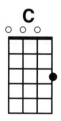	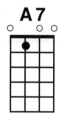	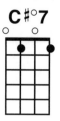

Baritone Ukulele

G	D7	G7	C	A7	C#°7
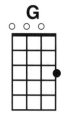	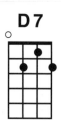	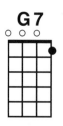	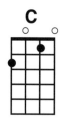		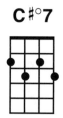

Guitar

G	D7	G7	C	A7	C#°7
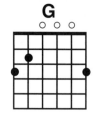	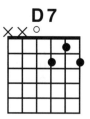	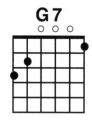	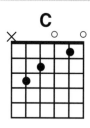	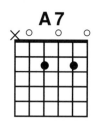	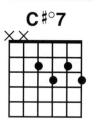

Mandolin

G	D7	G7	C	A7	C#°7
	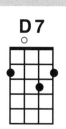	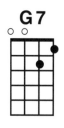	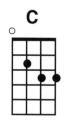		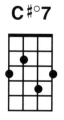

Banjo

G	D7	G7	C	A7	C#°7
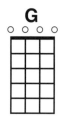	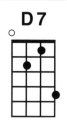	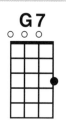	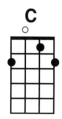	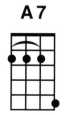	

Blue Christmas

Words and Music by Billy Hayes and Jay Johnson

13

Standard Ukulele

D	E m	A 7	A	G
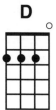	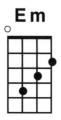	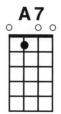		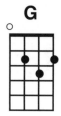

Baritone Ukulele

D	E m	A 7	A	G
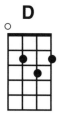	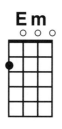		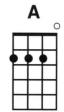	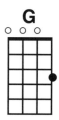

Guitar

D	E m	A 7	A	G
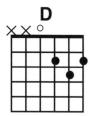	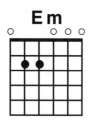	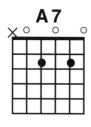	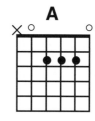	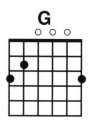

Mandolin

D	E m	A 7	A	G
	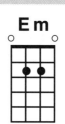		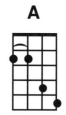	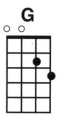

Banjo

D	E	A 7	A	G
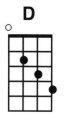	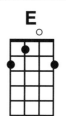			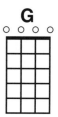

Christ Was Born on Christmas Day

Traditional

Verse

1. Christ was born on Christ - mas Day, wreath the hol - ly,
2. He is born to set us free, He is born our
3. Let the bright red ber - ries glow. Ev - 'ry - where in
4. Christ - ian men re - joice and sing. 'Tis the birth - day

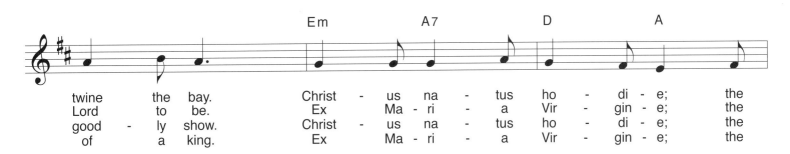

twine the bay. Christ - us na - tus ho - di - e; the
Lord to be. Ex Ma - ri - a Vir - gin - e; the
good - ly show. Christ - us na - tus ho - di - e; the
of a king. Ex Ma - ri - a Vir - gin - e; the

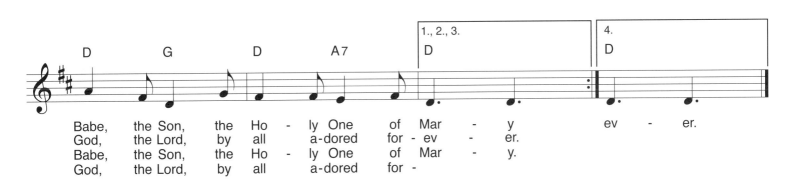

Babe, the Son, the Ho - ly One of Mar - y ev - er.
God, the Lord, by all a - dored for - ev - er.
Babe, the Son, the Ho - ly One of Mar - y.
God, the Lord, by all a - dored for -

Standard Ukulele

G 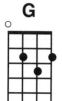 D 7  D sus4 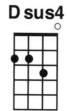 D 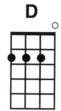 E m 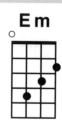 A 7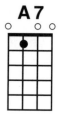

Baritone Ukulele

G 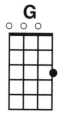 D 7 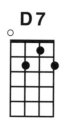 D sus4 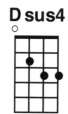 D 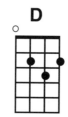 E m 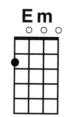 A 7

Guitar

G 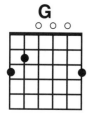 D 7 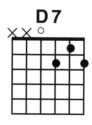 D sus4 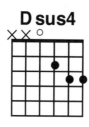 D 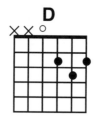 E m 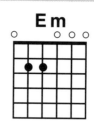 A 7

Mandolin

G 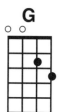 D 7 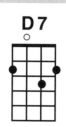 D sus4 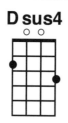 D 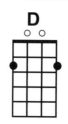 E m 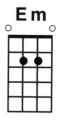 A 7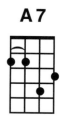

Banjo

G 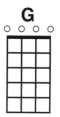 D 7 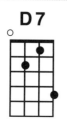 D sus4 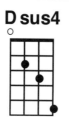 D 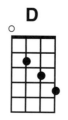 E m 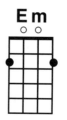 A 7

Deck the Hall

Traditional Welsh Carol

Standard Ukulele

C	Am	Em	F	G	E	Dm
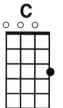	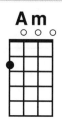	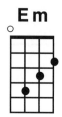			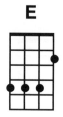	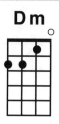

Baritone Ukulele

C	Am	Em	F	G	E	Dm
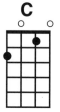	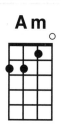	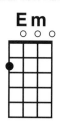		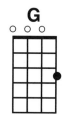	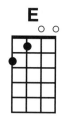	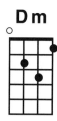

Guitar

C	Am	Em	F	G	E	Dm
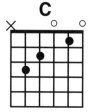	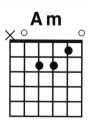	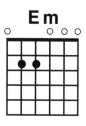	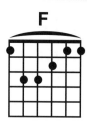	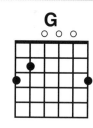	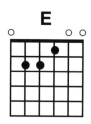	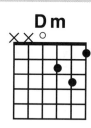

Mandolin

C	Am	Em	F	G	E	Dm
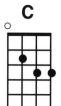	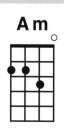	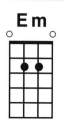	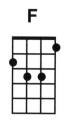	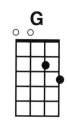	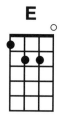	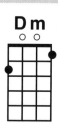

Banjo

C	Am	Em	F	G	E	Dm
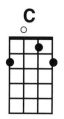	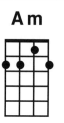	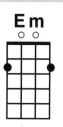		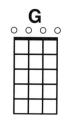	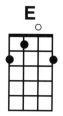	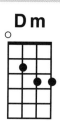

Do You Hear What I Hear

Words and Music by Noel Regney and Gloria Shayne

Standard Ukulele

G	A 7	D	B m
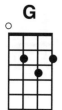	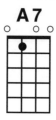	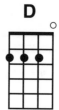	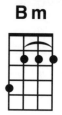

Baritone Ukulele

G	A 7	D	B m
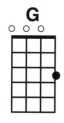		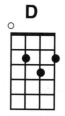	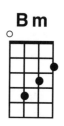

Guitar

G	A 7	D	B m
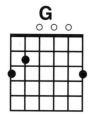	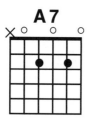	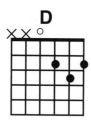	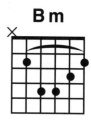

Mandolin

G	A 7	D	B m
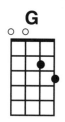	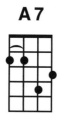	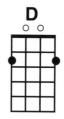	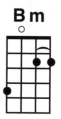

Banjo

G	A 7	D	B m
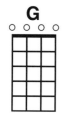		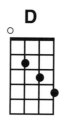	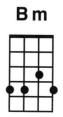

Feliz Navidad

Music and Lyrics by José Feliciano

Standard Ukulele

D	A	G	A 7	F♯m
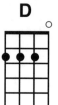	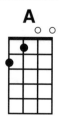	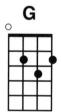	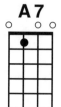	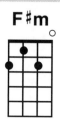

Baritone Ukulele

D	A	G	A 7	F♯m
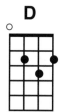	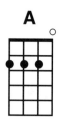	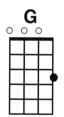		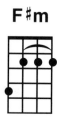

Guitar

D	A	G	A 7	F♯m
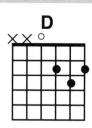	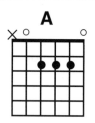	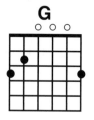		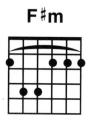

Mandolin

D	A	G	A 7	F♯m
	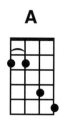	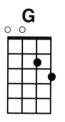	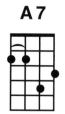	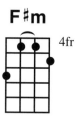 4fr

Banjo

D	A	G	A 7	F♯m
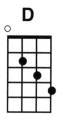		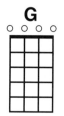	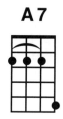	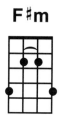

The First Noël

17th Century English Carol
Music from W. Sandy's Christmas Carols

Standard Ukulele

C	F	A 7	D m	G 7
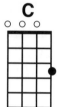	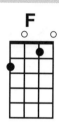	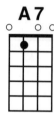	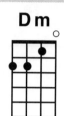	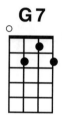

Baritone Ukulele

C	F	A 7	D m	G 7
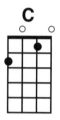		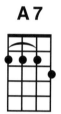	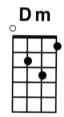	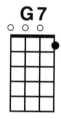

Guitar

C	F	A 7	D m	G 7
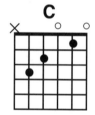	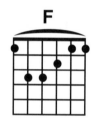		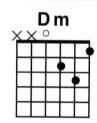	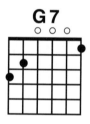

Mandolin

C	F	A 7	D m	G 7
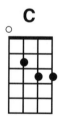		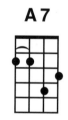	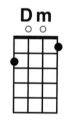	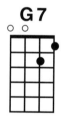

Banjo

C	F	A 7	D m	G 7
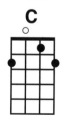	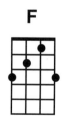		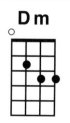	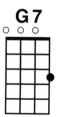

Frosty the Snow Man

Words and Music by Steve Nelson and Jack Rollins

Standard Ukulele

G	C	D 7	E m	A m	A 7

 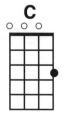  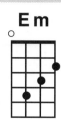 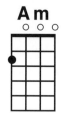 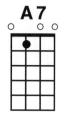

Baritone Ukulele

G	C	D 7	E m	A m	A 7

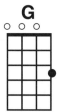 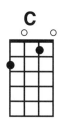 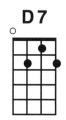 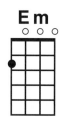 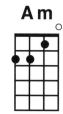 

Guitar

G	C	D 7	E m	A m	A 7

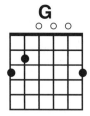 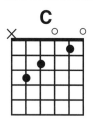 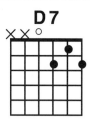 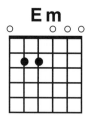  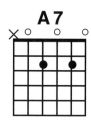

Mandolin

G	C	D 7	E m	A m	A 7

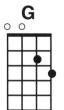 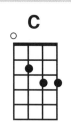  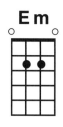 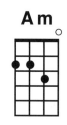 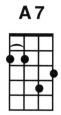

Banjo

G	C	D 7	E m	A m	A 7

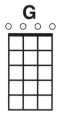 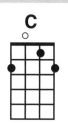 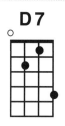 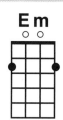  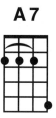

Go, Tell It on the Mountain

African-American Spiritual
Verses by John W. Work, Jr.

Chorus

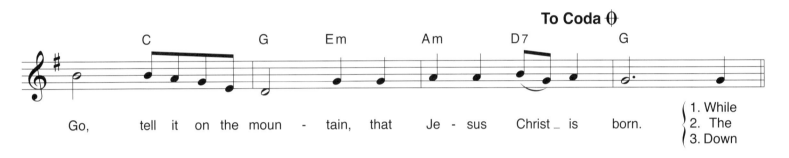

Go,   tell it on the moun - tain,   o - ver the hills and ev - 'ry - where.

To Coda ⊕

Go,   tell it on the moun - tain, that Je - sus Christ _ is born.

1. While
2. The
3. Down

Verse

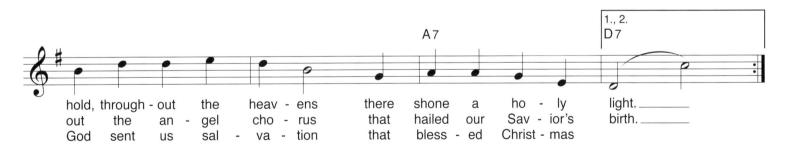

shep - herds kept   their watch - ing,   o'er si - lent flocks by night,   be -
shep - herds feared and trem - bled when, lo! a - bove the earth   rang
in   a low - ly man - ger   the hum - ble Christ was born,   and

1., 2.

hold, through - out the heav - ens there shone a ho - ly light.____
out the an - gel cho - rus that hailed our Sav - ior's birth.____
God sent us sal - va - tion that bless - ed Christ - mas

3.

D.C. al Coda

morn.____

⊕ Coda

born.

Standard Ukulele

E m	B 7	C	A m	G	D

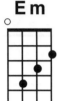  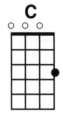 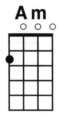 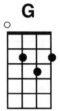 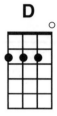

Baritone Ukulele

E m	B 7	C	A m	G	D

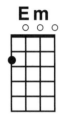 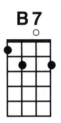 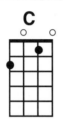 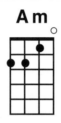 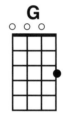 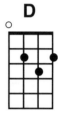

Guitar

E m	B 7	C	A m	G	D

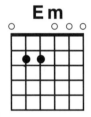 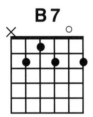 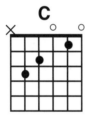  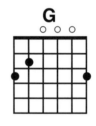 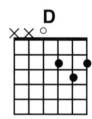

Mandolin

E m	B 7	C	A m	G	D

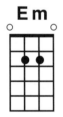 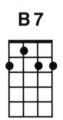 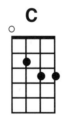 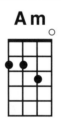 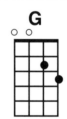 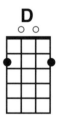

Banjo

E m	B 7	C	A m	G	D

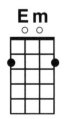 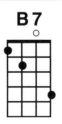 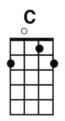 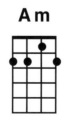 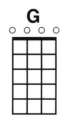 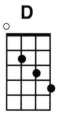

God Rest Ye Merry, Gentlemen

Traditional English Carol

Standard Ukulele

D	Em	A7	E7	A	Bm
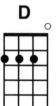	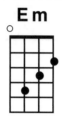	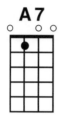	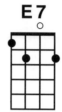	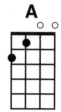	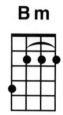

Baritone Ukulele

D	Em	A7	E7	A	Bm
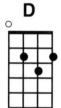	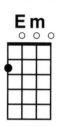	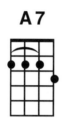	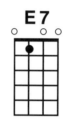	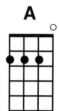	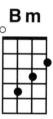

Guitar

D	Em	A7	E7	A	Bm
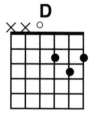	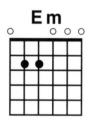	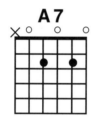	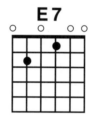	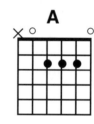	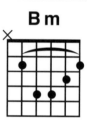

Mandolin

D	Em	A7	E7	A	Bm
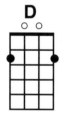	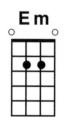	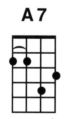	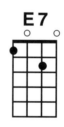	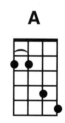	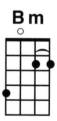

Banjo

D	E	A7	E7	A	Bm
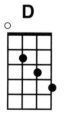	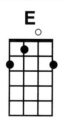	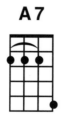	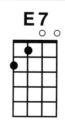	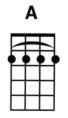	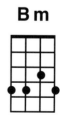

Happy Holiday

from the Motion Picture Irving Berlin's HOLIDAY INN
Words and Music by Irving Berlin

Standard Ukulele

G   Am    D7    C 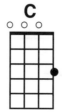   Dm 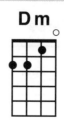   G7 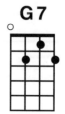   F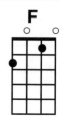

Baritone Ukulele

G 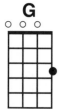   Am 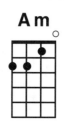   D7 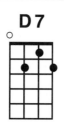   C 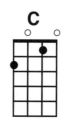   Dm 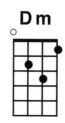   G7 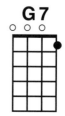   F

Guitar

G 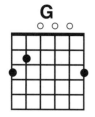   Am 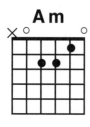   D7 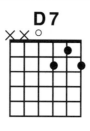   C 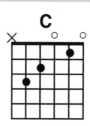   Dm 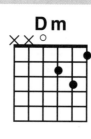   G7 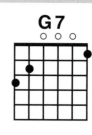   F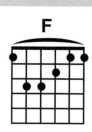

Mandolin

G 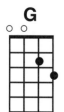   Am 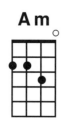   D7 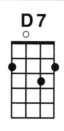   C 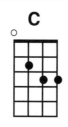   Dm 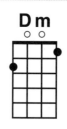   G7 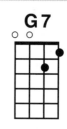   F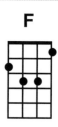

Banjo

G 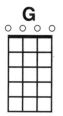   Am 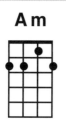   D7 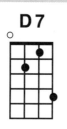   C 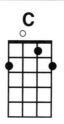   Dm 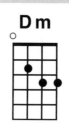   G7 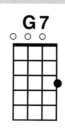   F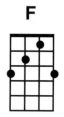

Happy Xmas
(War Is Over)
Written by John Lennon and Yoko Ono

Standard Ukulele

G 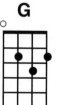 **D** 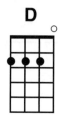 **C** 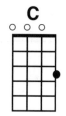 **Em** 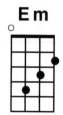 **A7** 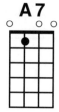 **E7** 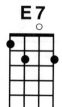 **Am**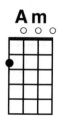

Baritone Ukulele

G 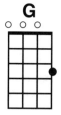 **D** 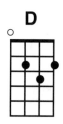 **C** 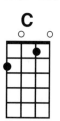 **Em** 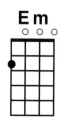 **A7**  **E7** 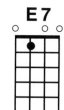 **Am**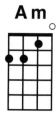

Guitar

G 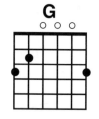 **D** 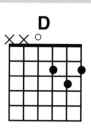 **C** 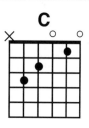 **Em** 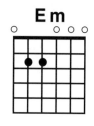 **A7**  **E7** 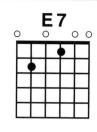 **Am**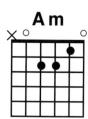

Mandolin

G 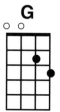 **D**  **C** 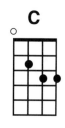 **Em**  **A7** 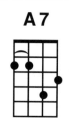 **E7** 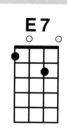 **Am**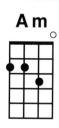

Banjo

G 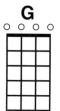 **D** 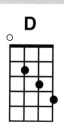 **C** 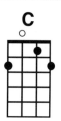 **Em** 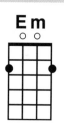 **A7**  **E7** 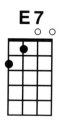 **Am**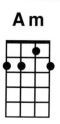

Hark! The Herald Angels Sing

Words by Charles Wesley
Altered by George Whitefield
Music by Felix Mendelssohn-Bartholdy

Standard Ukulele

D	A 7	D 7	G	G#○7	B 7	E m

 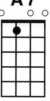

Baritone Ukulele

D	A 7	D 7	G	G#○7	B 7	E m

   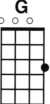   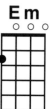

Guitar

D	A 7	D 7	G	G#○7	B 7	E m

 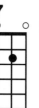   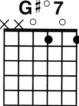 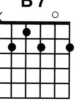 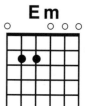

Mandolin

D	A 7	D 7	G	G#○7	B 7	E m

 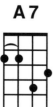 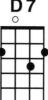 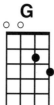 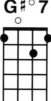 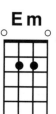

Banjo

D	A 7	D 7	G	G#○7	B 7	E m

Here Comes Santa Claus
(Right Down Santa Claus Lane)

Words and Music by Gene Autry and Oakley Haldeman

Standard Ukulele

G	C	D
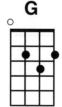	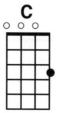	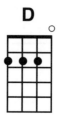

Baritone Ukulele

G	C	D
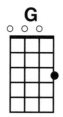	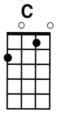	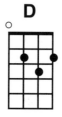

Guitar

G	C	D
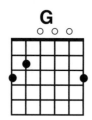	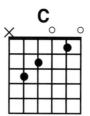	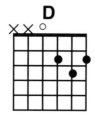

Mandolin

G	C	D
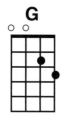	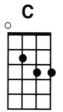	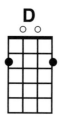

Banjo

G	C	D
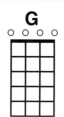	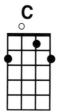	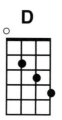

The Holly and the Ivy

18th Century English Carol

Standard Ukulele

C 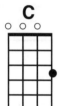 G 7 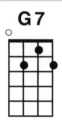 F 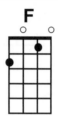 E m 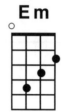 D m 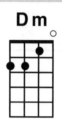 A m 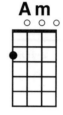 D 7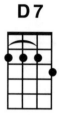

Baritone Ukulele

C 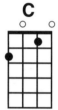 G 7 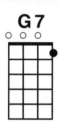 F 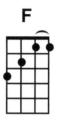 E m 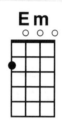 D m 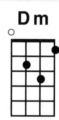 A m 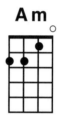 D 7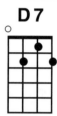

Guitar

C 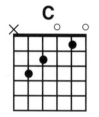 G 7 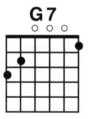 F  E m 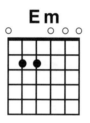 D m 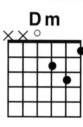 A m 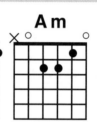 D 7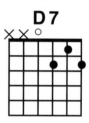

Mandolin

 C  G 7 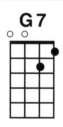 F  E m 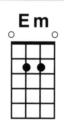 D m  A m 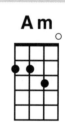 D 7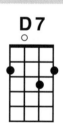

Banjo

C 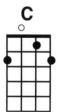 G 7 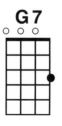 F 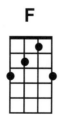 E m  D m 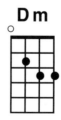 A m 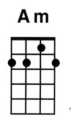 D 7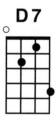

A Holly Jolly Christmas

Music and Lyrics by Johnny Marks

Standard Ukulele

C	F	A 7	D 7	G 7	C 7	G

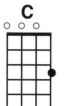 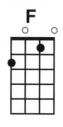 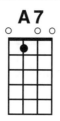  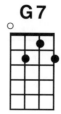 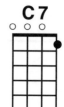 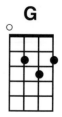

Baritone Ukulele

C	F	A 7	D 7	G 7	C 7	G

   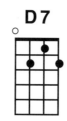 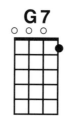  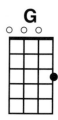

Guitar

C	F	A 7	D 7	G 7	C 7	G

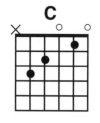 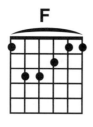 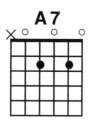 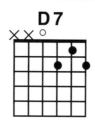 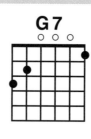 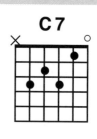 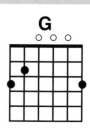

Mandolin

C	F	A 7	D 7	G 7	C 7	G

   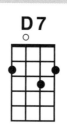 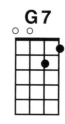 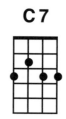 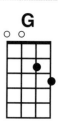

Banjo

C	F	A 7	D 7	G 7	C 7	G

  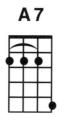 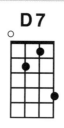 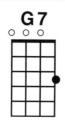 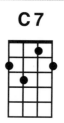 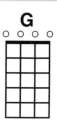

(There's No Place Like)
Home for the Holidays

Words and Music by Al Stillman and Robert Allen

Standard Ukulele

D	D#°7	A7	F°7	G	F#7	Bm

Baritone Ukulele

D	D#°7	A7	F°7	G	F#7	Bm

Guitar

D	D#°7	A7	F°7	G	F#7	Bm

   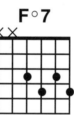 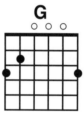  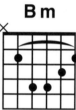

Mandolin

D	D#°7	A7	F°7	G	F#7	Bm

    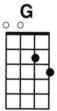 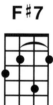 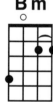

Banjo

D	D#°7	A7	F°7	G	F#7	Bm

   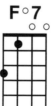 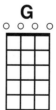

I Heard the Bells on Christmas Day

Words by Henry Wadsworth Longfellow
Music by John Baptiste Calkin

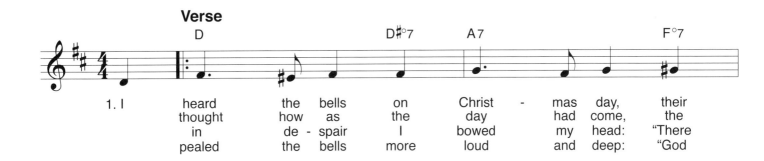

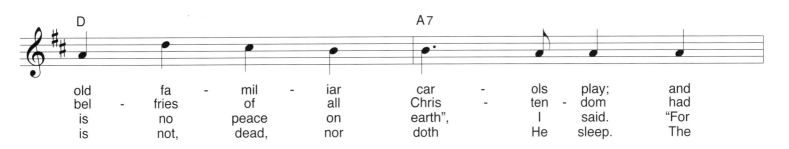

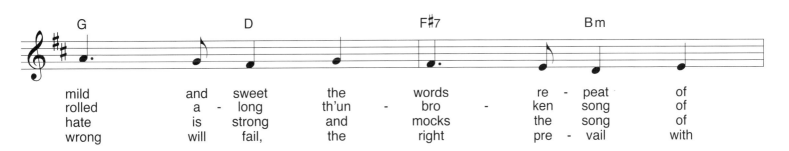

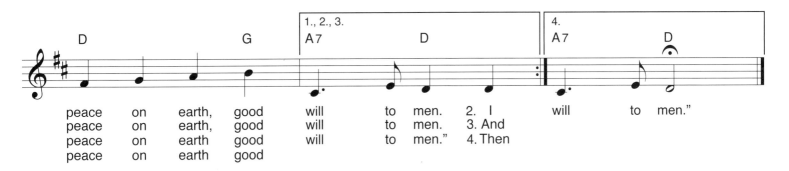

Standard Ukulele

Am 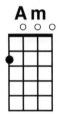 **Dm** 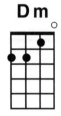 **Em**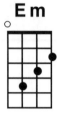

Baritone Ukulele

Am 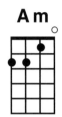 **Dm** 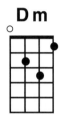 **Em**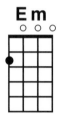

Guitar

Am  **Dm** 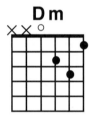 **Em**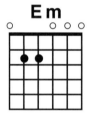

Mandolin

Am 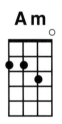 **Dm** 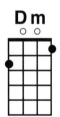 **Em**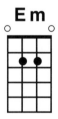

Banjo

Am 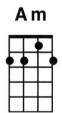 **Dm** 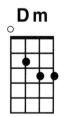 **Em**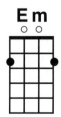

I Wonder As I Wander

By John Jacob Niles

Standard Ukulele

G	C	A 7	D	D 7	B 7	E m

 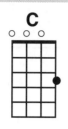 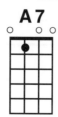 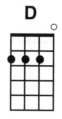  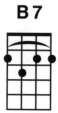 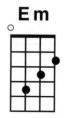

Baritone Ukulele

G	C	A 7	D	D 7	B 7	E m

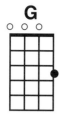 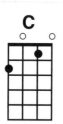  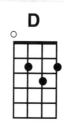 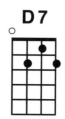  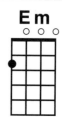

Guitar

G	C	A 7	D	D 7	B 7	E m

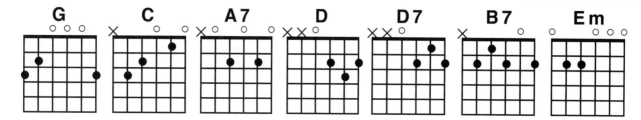

Mandolin

G	C	A 7	D	D 7	B 7	E m

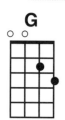 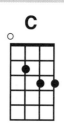 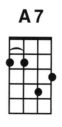 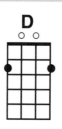 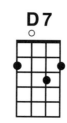 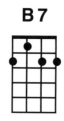 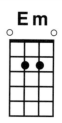

Banjo

G	C	A 7	D	D 7	B 7	E m

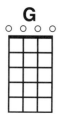 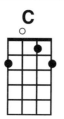 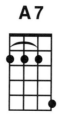 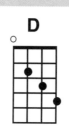 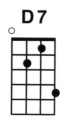 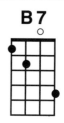 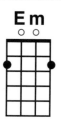

It Came Upon the Midnight Clear

Words by Edmund Hamilton Sears
Music by Richard Storrs Willis

Standard Ukulele

G 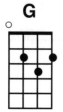   **C** 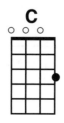   **Am** 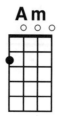   **D7** 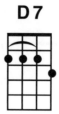   **A7**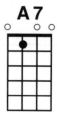

Baritone Ukulele

G 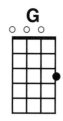   **C**    **Am** 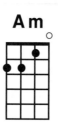   **D7** 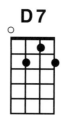   **A7**

Guitar

G 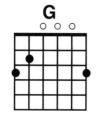   **C** 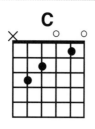   **Am** 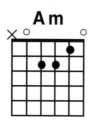   **D7** 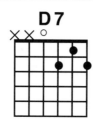   **A7**

Mandolin

G 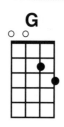   **C** 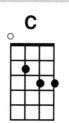   **Am** 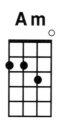   **D7**    **A7**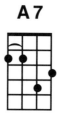

Banjo

G 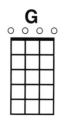   **C** 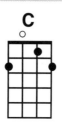   **Am** 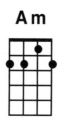   **D7** 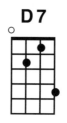   **A7**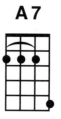

Jingle Bells

Words and Music by J. Pierpont

Standard Ukulele

G	D 7	E m	G 7	C	A 7

 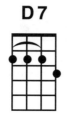 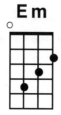 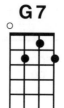 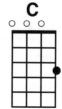 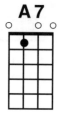

Baritone Ukulele

G	D 7	E m	G 7	C	A 7

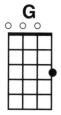 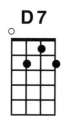 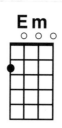 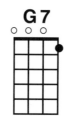  

Guitar

G	D 7	E m	G 7	C	A 7

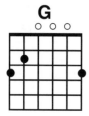 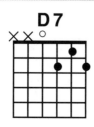 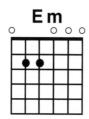 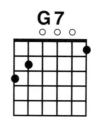 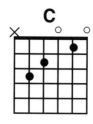 

Mandolin

G	D 7	E m	G 7	C	A 7

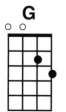 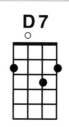 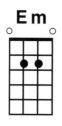 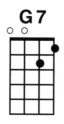 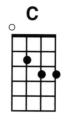 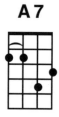

Banjo

G	D 7	E m	G 7	C	A 7

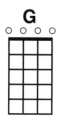 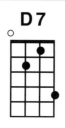 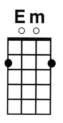 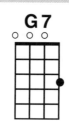 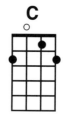 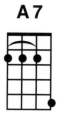

Jolly Old St. Nicholas

Traditional 19th Century American Carol

1. Jol - ly Old Saint Nich - o - las, lean your ear this way.
2. When the clock is strik - ing twelve, when I'm fast a - sleep.
3. John - ny wants a pair of skates; Su - zy wants a doll.

Don't you tell a sin - gle soul what I'm going to say.
Down the chim - ney broad and black, with your pack you'll creep.
Nel - lie wants a sto - ry book, she thinks dolls are fol - ly.

Christ - mas Eve is com - ing soon, now you dear old man,
All the stock - ings you will find hang - ing in a row.
As for me, my lit - tle brain is - n't ver - y bright.

whis - per what you'll bring to me; tell me if you can.
Mine will be the short - est one, you'll be sure to know.
Choose for me, old San - ta Claus, what you think is right.

Standard Ukulele

D	A 7	G
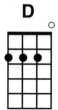	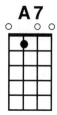	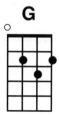

Baritone Ukulele

D	A 7	G
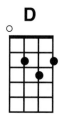	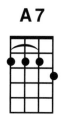	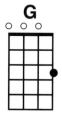

Guitar

D	A 7	G
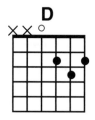	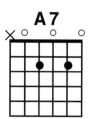	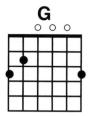

Mandolin

D	A 7	G
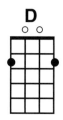	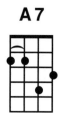	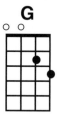

Banjo

D	A 7	G
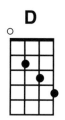	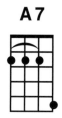	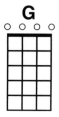

Joy to the World

Words by Isaac Watts
Music by George Frideric Handel
Adapted by Lowell Mason

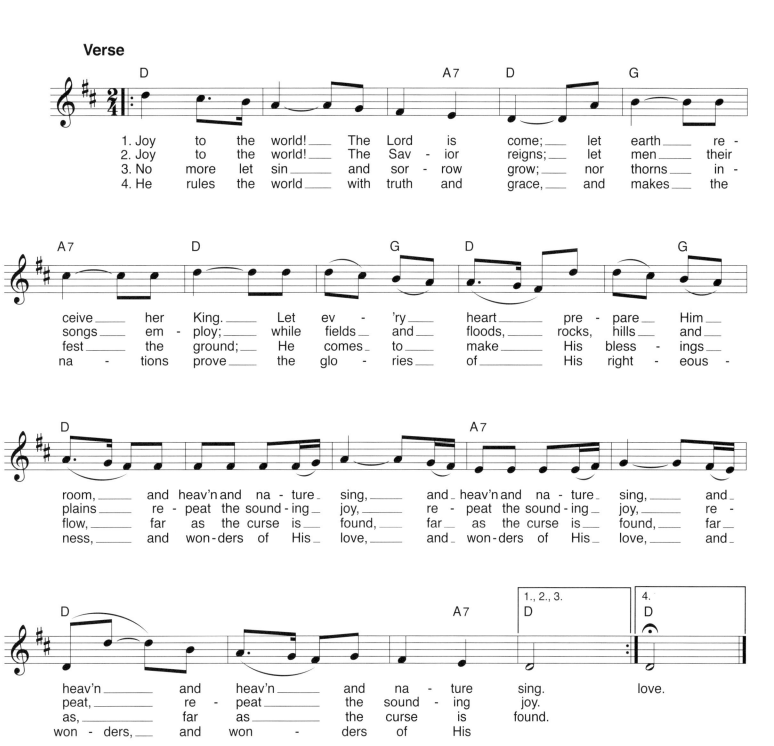

Standard Ukulele

G
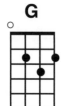

D
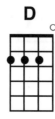

G 7
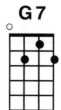

C
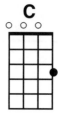

Baritone Ukulele

G
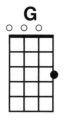

D
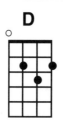

G 7
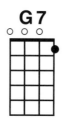

C
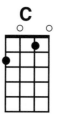

Guitar

G
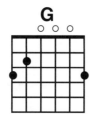

D
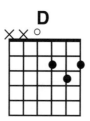

G 7
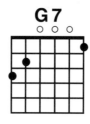

C
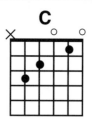

Mandolin

G
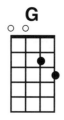

D
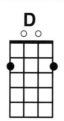

G 7
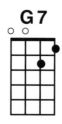

C
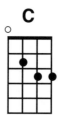

Banjo

G
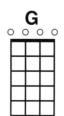

D
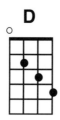

G 7
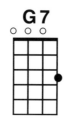

C
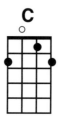

The Little Drummer Boy

Words and Music by Harry Simeone, Henry Onorati and Katherine Davis

Standard Ukulele

| D | F○7 | A 7 | E m | G | B 7 | E 7 |

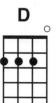  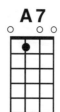 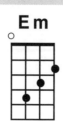 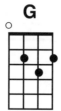  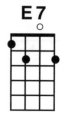

Baritone Ukulele

| D | F○7 | A 7 | E m | G | B 7 | E 7 |

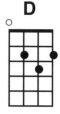 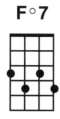 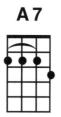 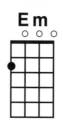 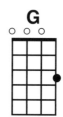 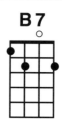 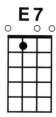

Guitar

| D | F○7 | A 7 | E m | G | B 7 | E 7 |

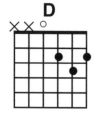 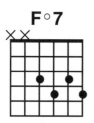 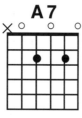 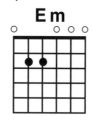 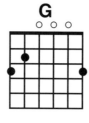 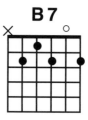 

Mandolin

| D | F○7 | A 7 | E m | G | B 7 | E 7 |

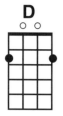  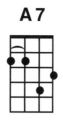  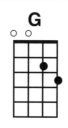  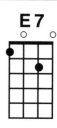

Banjo

| D | F○7 | A 7 | E m | G | B 7 | E 7 |

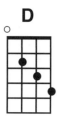 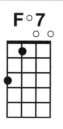  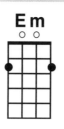 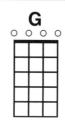 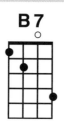 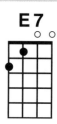

Mele Kalikimaka

Words and Music by R. Alex Anderson

Standard Ukulele

G	C	A 7	D 7	E m
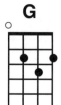	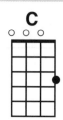	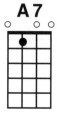		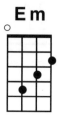

Baritone Ukulele

G	C	A 7	D 7	E m
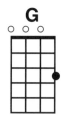	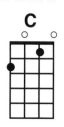		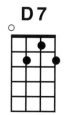	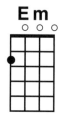

Guitar

G	C	A 7	D 7	E m
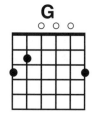	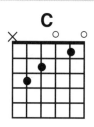	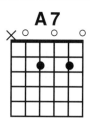	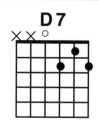	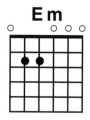

Mandolin

G	C	A 7	D 7	E m
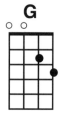	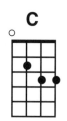	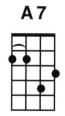	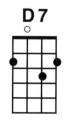	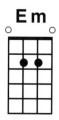

Banjo

G	C	A 7	D 7	E m
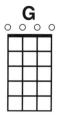	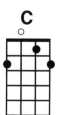		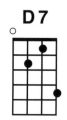	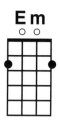

Nuttin' for Christmas

Words and Music by Roy C. Bennett and Sid Tepper

Standard Ukulele

G   D 7  A m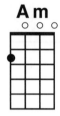

Baritone Ukulele

G 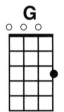 D 7 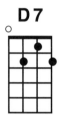 A m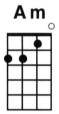

Guitar

G 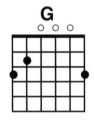 D 7 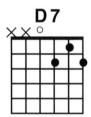 A m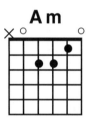

Mandolin

G 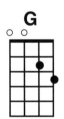 D 7 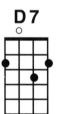 A m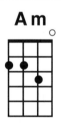

Banjo

G 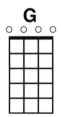 D 7 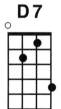 A m

O Christmas Tree

Traditional German Carol

Standard Ukulele

  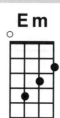

Baritone Ukulele

    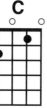 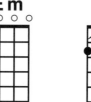

Guitar

 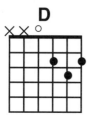  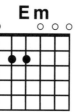 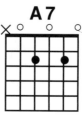 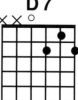

Mandolin

  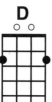 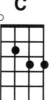 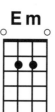 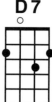

Banjo

O Come, All Ye Faithful

Music by John Francis Wade
Latin Words translated by Frederick Oakeley

Verse

1. O come, all ye faith - ful, jo - ful and tri -
2. Sing, choirs of an - gels, sing in ex - ul -
3. Yea, Lord, we greet Thee, born this hap - py

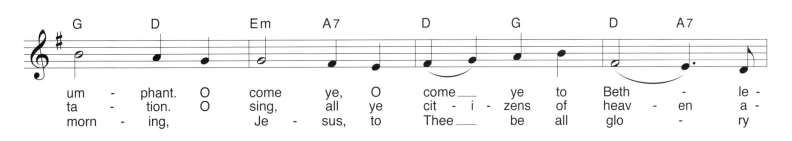

um - phant. O come ye, O come____ ye to Beth - le -
ta - tion. O sing, all ye cit - i - zens of heav - en a -
morn - ing, Je - sus, to Thee____ be all glo - ry

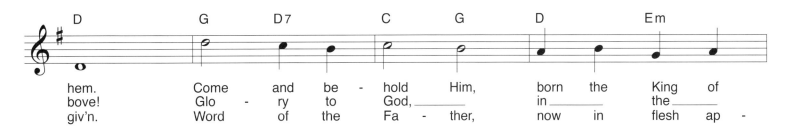

hem. Come and be - hold Him, born the King of
bove! Glo - ry to God,____ in____ the____
giv'n. Word of the Fa - ther, now in flesh ap -

Chorus

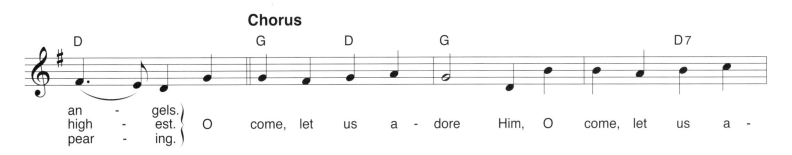

an - gels.
high - est. } O come, let us a - dore Him, O come, let us a -
pear - ing.

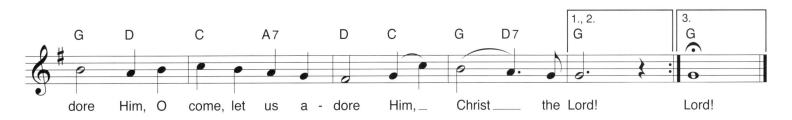

dore Him, O come, let us a - dore Him,__ Christ____ the Lord!   Lord!

Standard Ukulele

G	A m	D 7	E 7	B 7	E m
		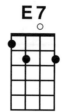		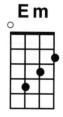	

Baritone Ukulele

G	A m	D 7	E 7	B 7	E m
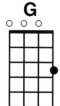	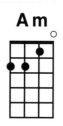	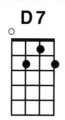	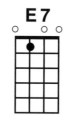	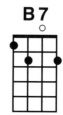	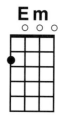

Guitar

G	A m	D 7	E 7	B 7	E m
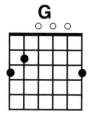	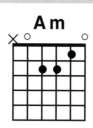	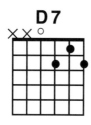	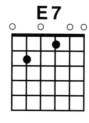	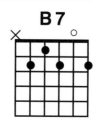	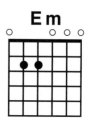

Mandolin

G	A m	D 7	E 7	B 7	E m
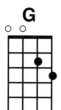	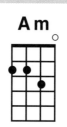	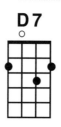	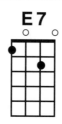	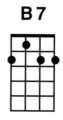	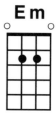

Banjo

G	A m	D 7	E 7	B 7	E m
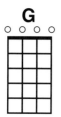	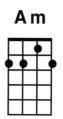	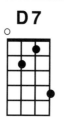	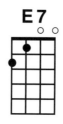	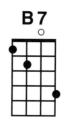	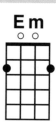

O Little Town of Bethlehem

Words by Phillips Brooks
Music by Lewis H. Redner

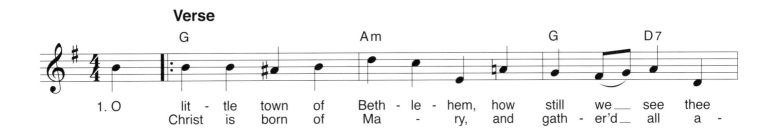

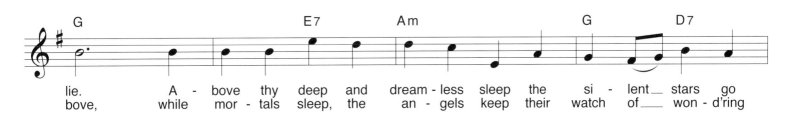

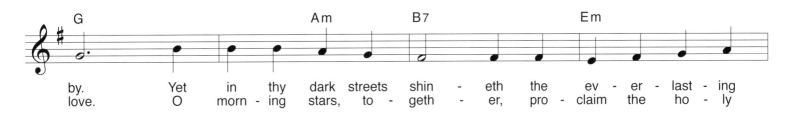

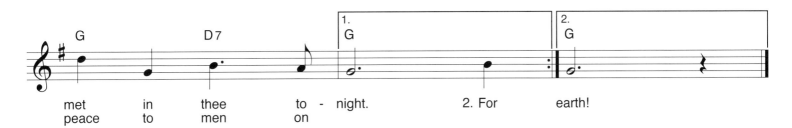

67

Standard Ukulele

C	G7	F	Em	Am	D7	Dm
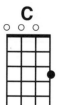	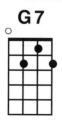		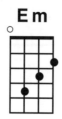	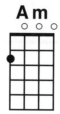		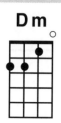

Baritone Ukulele

C	G7	F	Em	Am	D7	Dm
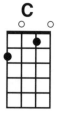	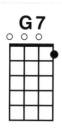		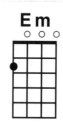	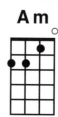	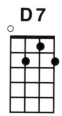	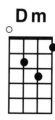

Guitar

C	G7	F	Em	Am	D7	Dm
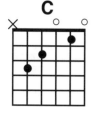	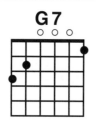	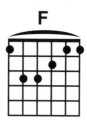	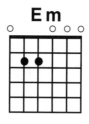		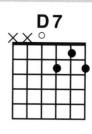	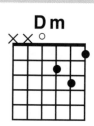

Mandolin

C	G7	F	Em	Am	D7	Dm
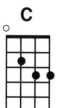	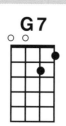	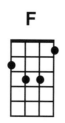	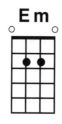	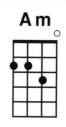	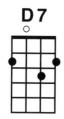	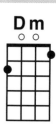

Banjo

C	G7	F	Em	Am	D7	Dm
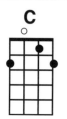	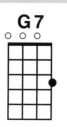		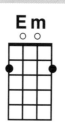	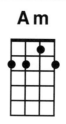	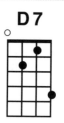	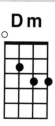

Rockin' Around the Christmas Tree

Music and Lyrics by Johnny Marks

Verse

C ... G7

1. Rock-in' a-round the Christ-mas tree __ at the Christ-mas par-ty hop. __
2. Rock-in' a-round the Christ-mas tree, __ let the Christ-mas spir-it ring. __
3. Rock-in' a-round the Christ-mas tree, __ have a hap-py hol-i-day. __

To Coda ⊕ *1.*

Mis-tle-toe hung where you can see __ ev-'ry cou-ple tries to
Lat-er we'll have some pump-kin pie __ and we'll
Ev-'ry-one danc-ing mer-ri-ly __ in the

C *2.* C

stop.   do some car-ol-ing.

Bridge

F ... Em

You will get a sen-ti-men-tal feel-ing when you hear

Am ... D7 N.C. ... G7 ... *D.C. al Coda*

voic-es sing-ing, "Let's be jol-ly. Deck the halls with boughs of hol-ly."

⊕ **Coda**

Dm ... G7 ... C

new old fash-ioned way. __

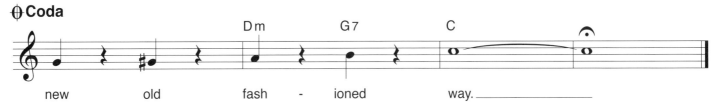

Standard Ukulele

C 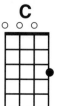 G7 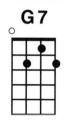 C7 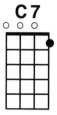 F 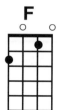 Am 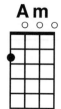 D7

Baritone Ukulele

C 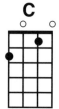 G7 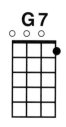 C7 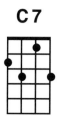 F  Am 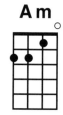 D7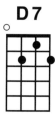

Guitar

C 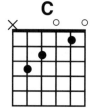 G7 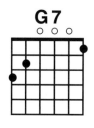 C7 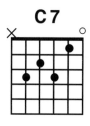 F 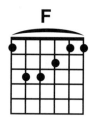 Am 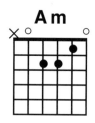 D7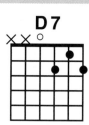

Mandolin

C 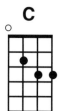 G7 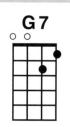 C7 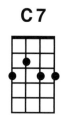 F  Am 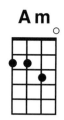 D7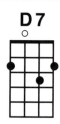

Banjo

C 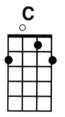 G7 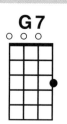 C7  F 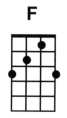 Am 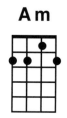 D7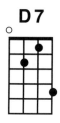

Rudolph the Red-Nosed Reindeer

Music and Lyrics by Johnny Marks

Standard Ukulele

C	F	Am	Dm	G7	D7	G
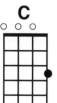		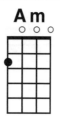	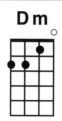	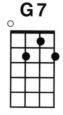		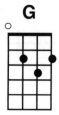

Baritone Ukulele

C	F	Am	Dm	G7	D7	G
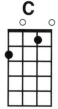		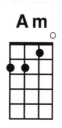		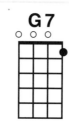	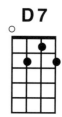	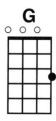

Guitar

C	F	Am	Dm	G7	D7	G
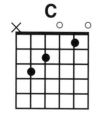			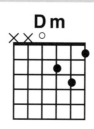	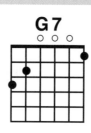	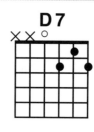	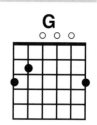

Mandolin

C	F	Am	Dm	G7	D7	G
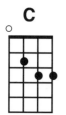		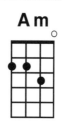	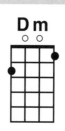	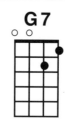	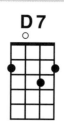	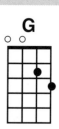

Banjo

C	F	Am	Dm	G7	D7	G
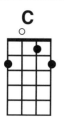			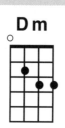	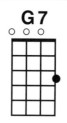	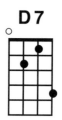	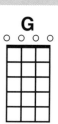

Santa Claus Is Comin' to Town

Words by Haven Gillespie
Music by J. Fred Coots

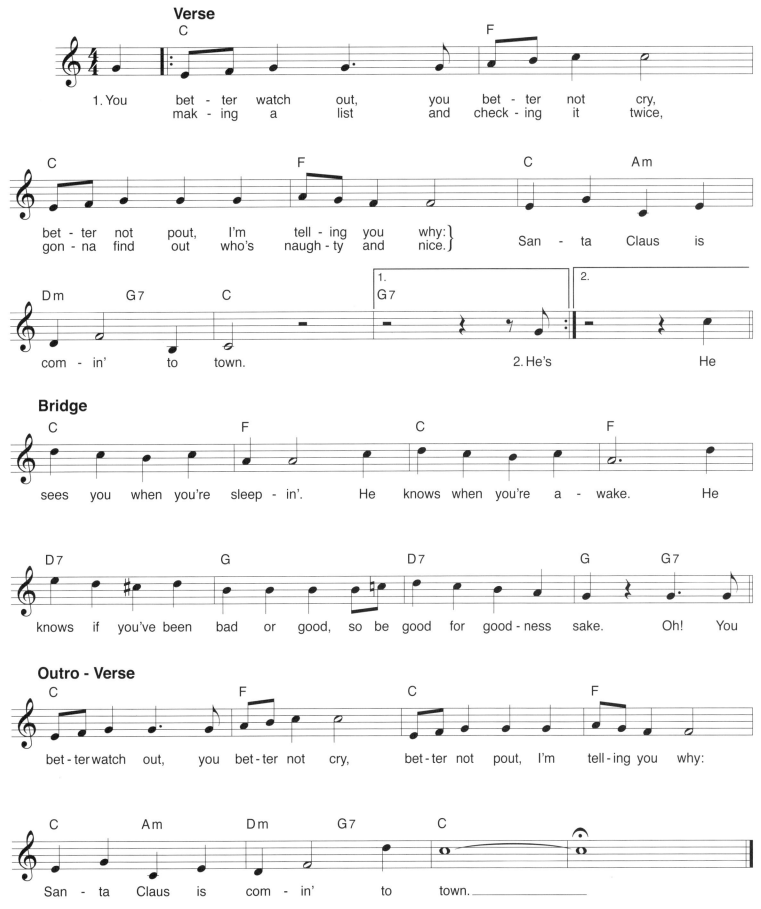

Standard Ukulele

G 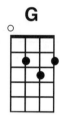 **D 7**  **C**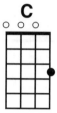

Baritone Ukulele

G 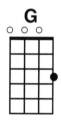 **D 7** 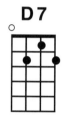 **C**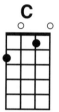

Guitar

G 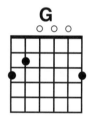 **D 7** 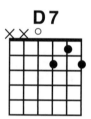 **C**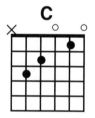

Mandolin

G 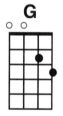 **D 7** 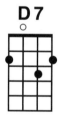 **C**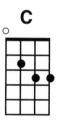

Banjo

G 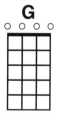 **D 7** 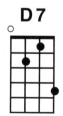 **C**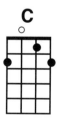

Silent Night

Words by Joseph Mohr
Translated by John F. Young
Music by Franz X. Gruber

Standard Ukulele

C	C7	F	Dm	G7
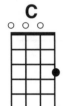	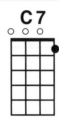	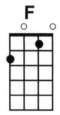	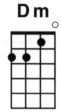	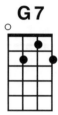

Baritone Ukulele

C	C7	F	Dm	G7
		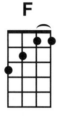	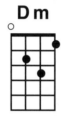	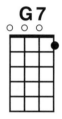

Guitar

C	C7	F	Dm	G7
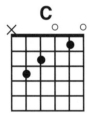	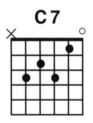	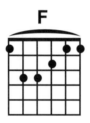	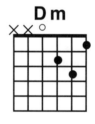	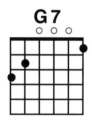

Mandolin

C	C7	F	Dm	G7
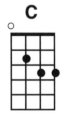	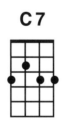	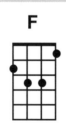	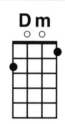	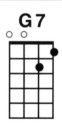

Banjo

C	C7	F	Dm	G7
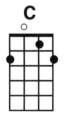	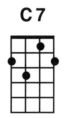	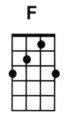	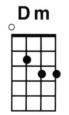	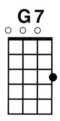

Silver Bells

from the Paramount Picture THE LEMON DROP KID
Words and Music by Jay Livingston and Ray Evans

Standard Ukulele

C	C#°7	Dm	G7	Am	F	D7

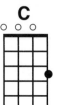 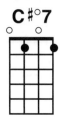 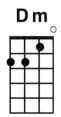 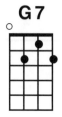 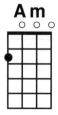  

Baritone Ukulele

C	C#°7	Dm	G7	Am	F	D7

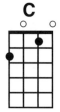  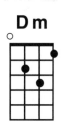 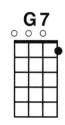 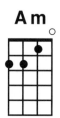  

Guitar

C	C#°7	Dm	G7	Am	F	D7

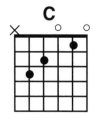 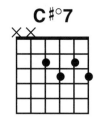 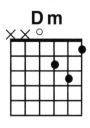 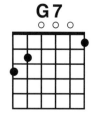  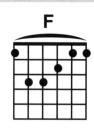 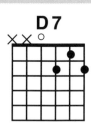

Mandolin

C	C#°7	Dm	G7	Am	F	D7

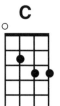 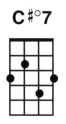 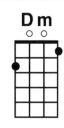 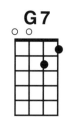 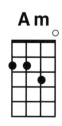  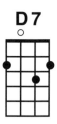

Banjo

C	C#°7	Dm	G7	Am	F	D7

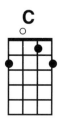 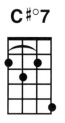 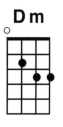 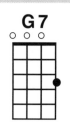 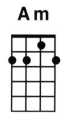  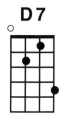

Suzy Snowflake

Words and Music by Sid Tepper and Roy Bennett

Standard Ukulele

G   **C**   **D 7**

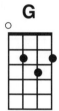 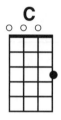 

Baritone Ukulele

G   **C**   **D 7**

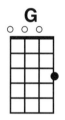  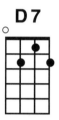

Guitar

G   **C**   **D 7**

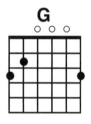 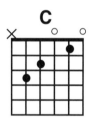 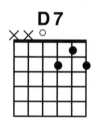

Mandolin

G   **C**   **D 7**

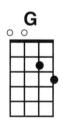 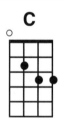 

Banjo

G   **C**   **D 7**

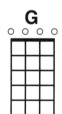 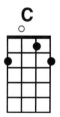 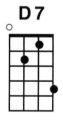

Up on the Housetop

Words and Music by B.R. Hanby

Standard Ukulele

Em	B7	D	G	Am	D7	C

  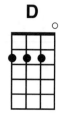 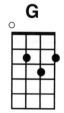 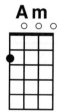  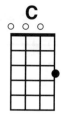

Baritone Ukulele

Em	B7	D	G	Am	D7	C

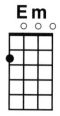 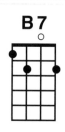 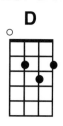 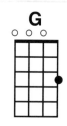 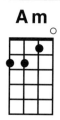 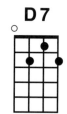 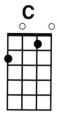

Guitar

Em	B7	D	G	Am	D7	C

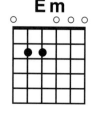 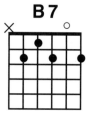 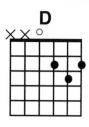 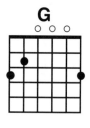  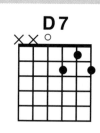 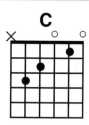

Mandolin

Em	B7	D	G	Am	D7	C

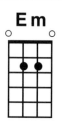 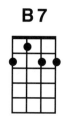 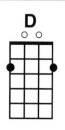 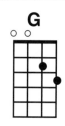 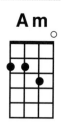 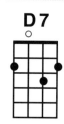 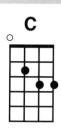

Banjo

Em	B7	D	G	Am	D7	C

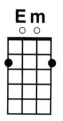 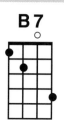 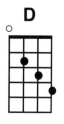 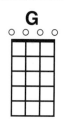 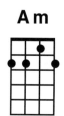 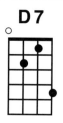 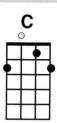

We Three Kings of Orient Are

Words and Music by John H. Hopkins, Jr.

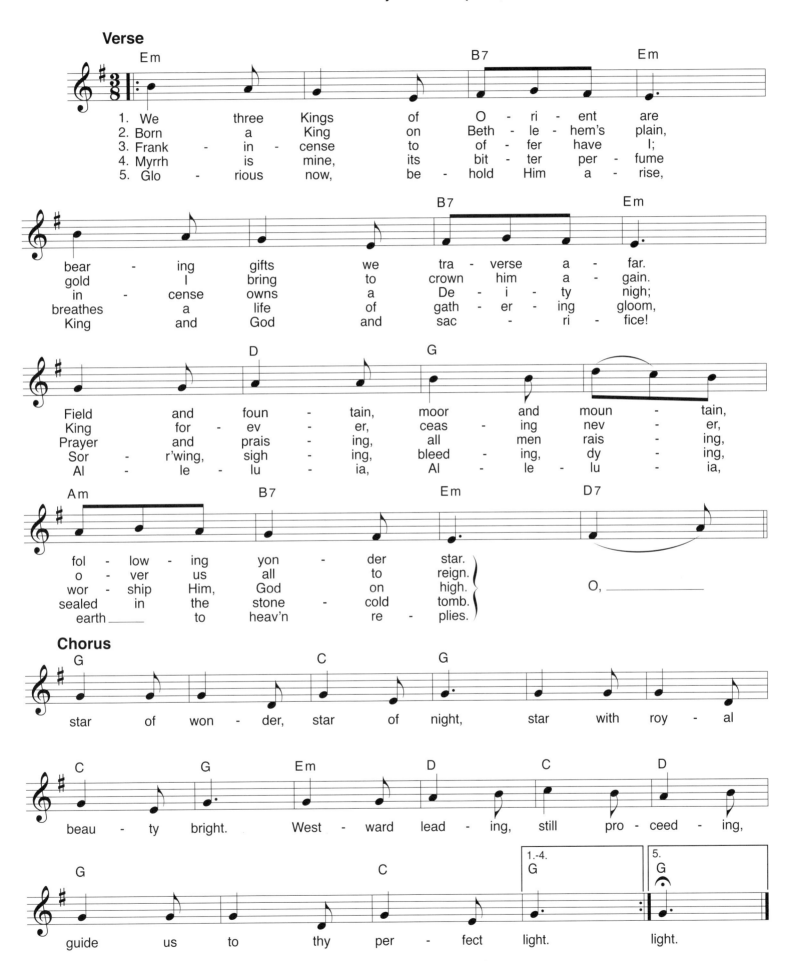

Standard Ukulele

G	C	A	D	B 7	E m	D 7
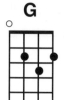	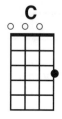	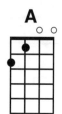	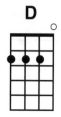		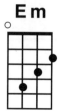	

Baritone Ukulele

G	C	A	D	B 7	E m	D 7
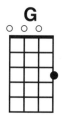	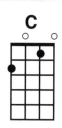	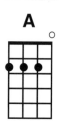	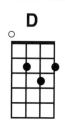	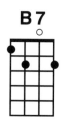	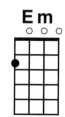	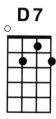

Guitar

G	C	A	D	B 7	E m	D 7
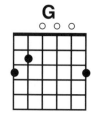	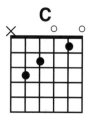	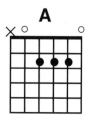	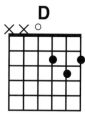	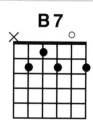	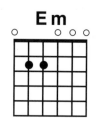	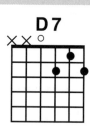

Mandolin

G	C	A	D	B 7	E m	D 7
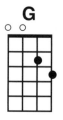	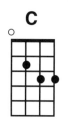	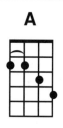	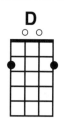		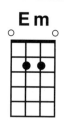	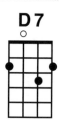

Banjo

G	C	A	D	B 7	E m	D 7
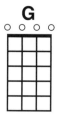	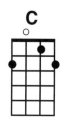		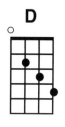	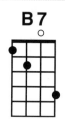	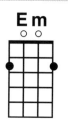	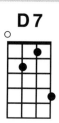

We Wish You a Merry Christmas

Traditional English Folksong

Standard Ukulele

F   C7   G7   A   E7   C   D7

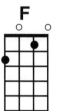 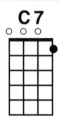 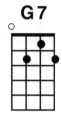 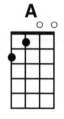 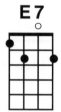 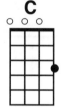 

Baritone Ukulele

F   C7   G7   A   E7   C   D7

 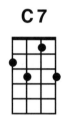 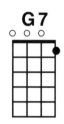 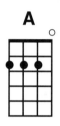 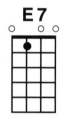 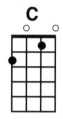 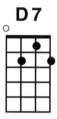

Guitar

F   C7   G7   A   E7   C   D7

 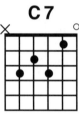 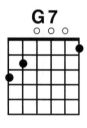 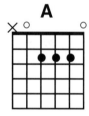  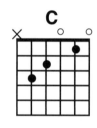 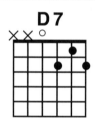

Mandolin

F   C7   G7   A   E7   C   D7

 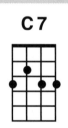 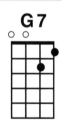 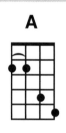 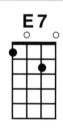 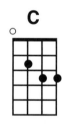 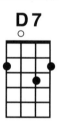

Banjo

F   C7   G7   A   E7   C   D7

  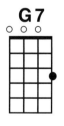 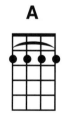 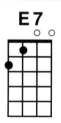 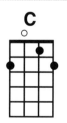 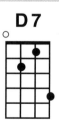

Winter Wonderland

Words by Dick Smith
Music by Felix Bernard